KU-685-121

— CHARITIES SERIES —
Editor: Roger J. Owen

SHELTER

£2, 25

David G. Kibble

DERBYSHIRE
SAINT BENEDICT
SCHOOL
COUNTY COUNCIL
MAY 1991

RMEP

RELIGIOUS AND MORAL EDUCATION PRESS
An Imprint of Arnold-Wheaton

Religious and Moral Education Press
An Imprint of Arnold-Wheaton
Hennock Road, Exeter EX2 8RP

Pergamon Press Ltd
Headington Hill Hall, Oxford OX3 0BW

Pergamon Press Inc.
Maxwell House, Fairview Park, Elmsford, New York 10523

Pergamon Press Canada Ltd
Suite 104, 150 Consumers Road, Willowdale, Ontario M2J 1P9

Pergamon Press (Australia) Pty Ltd
P.O. Box 544, Potts Point, N.S.W. 2011

Pergamon Press GmbH
Hammerweg 6, D-6242 Kronberg, Federal Republic of Germany

Copyright © 1983 David G. Kibble

*All rights reserved. No part of this publication
may be reproduced, stored in a retrieval system,
or transmitted, in any form or by any means,
electronic, electrostatic, magnetic tape,
mechanical, photocopying, recording or otherwise,
without permission in writing from the publishers.*

First published 1983
Reprinted 1984

Illustrated by Delphine Jones

Printed in Great Britain by A. Wheaton & Co. Ltd, Exeter (*W*)
ISBN 0 08-025635-X non net
ISBN 0 08-025636-8 net

Foreword

Shelter is a charity, but not a normal one. It deals with no ordinary problem. Lack of a decent home can harm a child's future, a pensioner's last years, or a young couple's marriage.

Shelter is a campaign. It aims to get rid of the evils of slum housing, to educate the next generation and give them a better chance in life, and to provide hope for the homeless where there was only despair.

Over the years Shelter has been a young people's campaign. The involvement of unpaid helpers of all ages, particularly young people, has been essential. These people have performed wonders. They have raised huge sums of money, put constant pressure on local councils and provided housing aid services in their spare time. In many cases, they have taken people in urgent need into their own homes. It is they who have provided the special character of Shelter over the years, and it is to them that this very useful book on the work of Shelter should be dedicated.

Neil McIntosh
Director, Shelter

Acknowledgements

The author and publishers would like to thank the following for permission to reproduce photographs in this book.
Daily Mirror: p. 9
S. R. Dewhurst: pp. 28, 29
Shelter Photo Library: pp. 12, 14, 16, 17, 20, 22, 24, 34
Shelter Photo Library/Ian Forsyth: pp. 7, 21, 31
Vollans of Knaresborough: p. 27

Contents

1

The Beginning of Shelter

'You make me totally sick. Kindly do not dish out trash on the BBC for an idiot mob such as Shelter.' So read a telegram that was sent to a television presenter who made an appeal on behalf of Shelter, the charity which tries to help the homeless. The sender of the telegram obviously had little sympathy for the thousands of families who are homeless or living in bad conditions.

One of the aims of Shelter is to make those of us who have good homes aware that not everyone is as fortunate as we are.

Cathy Come Home

Shelter was formed on 1 December 1966. Five major charities helped to start it off. They were the Housing Societies Fund Charitable Trust, Christian Action, Housing the Homeless Central Fund, British Churches Housing Trust and the Catholic Housing Aid Society. It was deliberately

A hostel for the homeless, St Albans

started at Christmas to take advantage of people's generosity and goodwill at that time of year. It was also hoped that people would realize what a sharp contrast there was between a happy family opening its presents on Christmas Day and the total misery of the homeless and people living in slums.

To start with, Shelter wanted to convey to people one important fact. This was that 3 million families in Britain lived in slums or in very overcrowded conditions.

Number of homeless households (England)

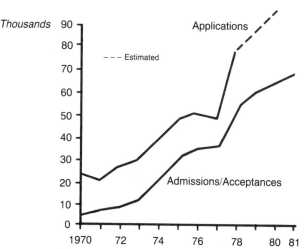

Administrative changes have increased the numbers of households recognized as homeless, but the underlying trend shows the problem of homelessness has not been tackled. In 1982 there were 157 000 applications and 73 600 admissions.
Source: Shelter.

A few days before Shelter began, something happened quite by accident. A play called *Cathy Come Home* was shown on television. The play, which was based on real events and real people, was about a homeless mother trying to keep her family together. It touched the hearts and consciences of the nation. Des Wilson, Shelter's first Director, said that the play 'made sure that the voice of Shelter was not only heard at the beginning of December, but understood'.

In four days Shelter had raised £7 000. In five it had raised £10 000. A full-page advertisement in *The Times* brought in an extra £12 000. At the end of the first week a news-sheet was produced and sent to 25 000 churches. That resulted in a further £10 000 being sent in.

Cathy Come Home was shown again in January 1967. Des Wilson and the play's author, Jeremy Sandford, talked about the homeless on *The Frost Programme* the same evening. So more and more people were learning of the work of Shelter.

At about two o'clock the following afternoon Des Wilson received a telephone call. It was from a man who said that he had just made his house into two flats and he was willing to offer one of them to any family Des Wilson named. Only minutes later a woman came into the Shelter office.

The Minchin family living in a tent in Halifax after eviction from their council house

9

She burst into tears. She explained, in between crying and sipping a cup of tea, that she and her husband were to be evicted the next day. Why? Because she was pregnant. The landlord did not want children in his flat. 'We've got to be out by tomorrow,' she said. 'I've been everywhere looking for a place. You're the first man to offer me anything, even a cup of tea.' Des Wilson remembered the man who had telephoned. He rang him back. Yes, he would be delighted to accept the couple.

During the next summer, thousands of young people organized sponsored walks for Shelter. At Christmas, BBC's *Blue Peter* programme made an appeal for stamps for the charity. All this helped Shelter to raise £200 000 in just over a year.

Shelter gave most of this money to housing associations. Housing associations are groups of local people who buy houses, which they repair or alter to make good, simple homes. Then they let the homes at reasonable rents to families in need. (The associations do not make a profit out of this.) In this way, Shelter enabled 1000 people to find homes.

In addition, Shelter continually brought to people's attention the terrible conditions of the homeless by informing the press of its work. It sent speakers to about 350 meetings. It showed *Cathy Come Home* over 400 times to youth groups, luncheon clubs, Rotary Clubs and other interested groups.

After the first year

Since that first year, Shelter has developed and changed. In October 1968 the Shelter Neighbourhood Action Project was set up in Liverpool to try to improve the living conditions of a whole community in a 'twilight zone' of the city. A 'twilight zone' is a decaying slum area, usually just outside the city centre.

In 1970 Shelter's Housing Aid Centre opened in London to help people with housing problems. For example, it gave advice to tenants who had bad landlords. It advised families on what to do about payment of rent if the bread-winner lost his job.

In 1972 a Youth Education Programme was launched to make school pupils aware of housing problems. A wide range of materials for the class-room, from small pamphlets to films and games, has been produced. Shelter believes that the next generation must be more able to help itself with its housing problems.

2

Without a Good Home

How do people become homeless?

The main cause of homelessness is trouble within the family. This accounts for nearly 40 per cent of the homeless. For example, parents might have a daughter and her husband living with them. The daughter becomes pregnant and has a child. The baby cries a lot. After many arguments the parents turn the young couple and the baby out of their home.

When a person buys a home of his own he usually borrows a large proportion of the money from a building society. This money is called a mortgage. He then pays back an amount each month which usually includes part of the original loan plus interest, although he may start by just paying off the interest. A person who loses his job may be unable to pay his mortgage repayment each month, although he can claim supplementary benefit from the D.H.S.S. which includes a fixed amount towards payment of the interest on a mortgage. If he is unable to meet his repayments the building society which loaned the money usually takes back the house from the family, who are then homeless.

Reasons for homelessness

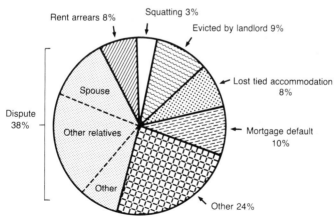

Source: *Social Trends*, H.M.S.O., 1979

11

With jobs becoming harder to find, many people are moving away from their own areas to find work. Perhaps in the town they left they had a council house, but once they move to another town they have to go to the bottom of the housing list.

Council housing

About one third of the population in the U.K. lives in council housing. Unfortunately, there are not enough council houses. In 1979 there were more than a million families on council-house waiting-lists. Slum-clearance families, large families and those who have lived in the area for a long time are usually considered first. Single people and one-parent families are often considered last of all, which means they may have a long wait.

Because of money problems, local councils have been building fewer council houses. Since 1975 the number being built each year has fallen. In 1981 only 20 592 were built, compared with 173 800 in 1975.

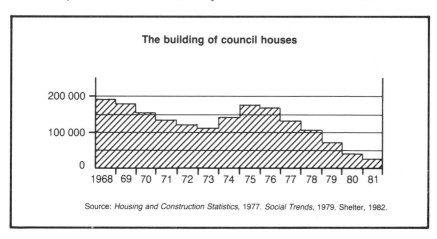

The building of council houses

Source: *Housing and Construction Statistics*, 1977. *Social Trends*, 1979. Shelter, 1982.

In 1979 the Conservative Government decided that people who lived in council houses could, if they wanted to, buy them from the council. This, of course, reduces the number of council houses available to rent. Shelter believes that the sale of council houses should be stopped unless a council can show that there is nobody waiting for a council house.

Private rented accommodation

Most people, when they leave home, do not have the money to pay for a deposit on a house. (A deposit is usually necessary before a building society will grant a mortgage.) They cannot get a council house straight away either. They therefore rent a furnished or unfurnished flat or house owned by a landlord.

Some of this housing is very poor: 40 per cent of all the unfit housing in Britain is owned by private landlords. They do not bother to do repairs and they ignore complaints. Most tenants do not know their rights. For example, a landlord cannot evict tenants without permission from a court. 13

Helen Ewart has no hot-water supply other than what she can heat on the stove and carry in this heavy boiler

Another problem is the recent heavy increase in rents. In Leeds, for example, a flat costing £30 a month in 1976 cost £88 a month in 1982. In London a small bed-sitter (a single room in which to live and sleep) might cost anything up to £40 a week. These high prices are due to the fact that more people want to rent a home but there are fewer flats and houses to rent.

In 1951, 54 per cent of all homes in Britain were rented by private landlords. By 1981 the figure was only 13½ per cent. The decline is due to three things.

First, landlords are finding it too costly to buy and look after such housing. Secondly, tenants have more rights under various Rent Acts and this has made landlords more cautious about letting property. For example, the 1965 Rent Act allows a tenant to appeal to a Rent Tribunal if he feels that his rent is too high, and the landlord has to accept the decision of the Tribunal. Thirdly, slum clearance has meant that many buildings owned by landlords have been knocked down.

Types of housing in Britain

Type of accommodation	1967 %	1969 %	1971 %	1973 %	1975 %	1977 %	1978 %	1979 %	1980 %
Owner occupied	47·9	49·4	50·5	52·3	53·0	53·6	55·9	56·5	57·3
Rented from local authority or new town	29·2	30·0	30·6	30·5	31·3	31·9	29·7	29·6	29·3
Rented from private landlord	22·9	20·6	18·9	17·2	15·7	14·5	14·4	13·9	13·4

Source: *Annual Abstract of Statistics*, H.M.S.O.

The results

One of the results of these facts is that it is becoming more difficult for poorer people to find a home. Even those who do manage to find housing often live in very bad conditions. In 1980, 62 420 families were homeless. In 1977, 700 000 families lived in conditions officially described as 'unfit for human living'. A further million had no bath, no hot water and no inside toilet. Another million homes needed major repairs.

Living in poor housing conditions damages health. Children are more likely to be ill. The constant strain from overcrowding, noise and rows between parents also leads to children having mental illnesses and conditions such as skin trouble, stuttering and being unable to concentrate.

An inability to concentrate means that children do not do well at school. This is also true if the child lives in a house where there is nowhere to do homework, or where he cannot sleep because of continual noise from other members of the family in the same room. A recent report showed that at the age of seven, children living in overcrowded homes were, on average, three months behind on reading. Those living in houses without proper facilities, such as an inside toilet, bath and hot tap, were nine months behind.

There are still houses without bathrooms

Bad housing also drives children out to play on the streets. The alternative is to stay indoors, probably watching television, and get in their mother's way. Once on the streets it is not long before the child gets into trouble with the police.

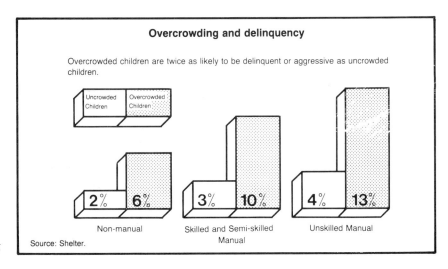

Overcrowding and delinquency

Overcrowded children are twice as likely to be delinquent or aggressive as uncrowded children.

| Uncrowded Children | Overcrowded Children |

| 2% | 6% | 3% | 10% | 4% | 13% |

Non-manual · Skilled and Semi-skilled Manual · Unskilled Manual

Source: Shelter.

When the child grows older he is likely to find life difficult. He comes out of school with few examination passes, if any, and has to take a job with a low wage, if he can find employment at all. Because of the insecurity of his childhood, he finds it difficult to get on with other people and cannot deal with problems. He is likely to marry someone from a similar background, which means that the marriage will probably be shaky.

Bad housing has a serious effect on children

S-A**

Adults suffer too. The parents have no pride in their home. Mother shouts at the children for being always under her feet. She becomes more irritable because they are ill so often and need looking after. The house cannot be kept clean. There is always the threat that the local authority might take the children into care, then the family would be split up. Father may be tempted to drink his way out of his misery and stay away from home; Mother will then feel neglected and depressed. In these conditions normal family life is difficult, even impossible. The temptation to run away or to commit suicide is often not far away.

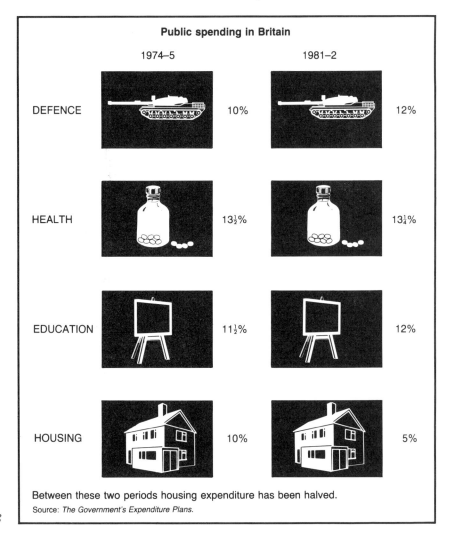

Public spending in Britain

	1974–5		1981–2	
DEFENCE		10%		12%
HEALTH		$13\frac{1}{2}$%		$13\frac{1}{4}$%
EDUCATION		$11\frac{1}{2}$%		12%
HOUSING		10%		5%

Between these two periods housing expenditure has been halved.

Source: *The Government's Expenditure Plans.*

3
Shelter at Work

Aiding housing associations

In its early days most of the money raised by Shelter was given to housing associations. Shelter decided to help associations in four cities where the need was greatest: London, Birmingham, Liverpool and Glasgow.

One housing association helped was the Notting Hill Housing Trust in London. In the late 1960s Notting Hill was a district consisting of three-, four- and five-storey Victorian terraced houses. These were owned by landlords who would let the large rooms in them, so each house was lived in by more than one family. This is known as 'multiple occupation'.

Shelter noted that the area showed all the usual signs of multiple occupation and decay: 'mouldering brickwork, chunks of stone missing from the steps, streets littered, pavements uneven . . . rusty, battered and overflowing dustbins, lidless dustbins covered with flies, scattered milk bottles, broken glass on roads and pavements, broken windows, lavatory doors missing, derelict cars and old furniture dumped in the streets'. The families living in the area were told that they would have to wait about ten years for a council house.

The Notting Hill Housing Trust, using money from Shelter, repaired a number of houses and let them to families in need in the area. In 1964 the Trust owned five houses. By February 1970 aid from Shelter meant that over 1500 people had been rehoused. By early 1979 the Trust owned 202 houses.

Shelter reports

The full name of Shelter is 'The Shelter National Campaign for the Homeless'. Shelter seeks to *campaign* for the homeless. It shouts on behalf of those least able to shout. One of the ways in which it does this is by publishing frequent reports. These are often taken up by the press and by television programmes such as *Nationwide*. Example of such reports are:

Housing and Campaigning   A report on the housing issues of the 1980s, describing campaigning techniques and how to use them for effective local campaigns.

Bringing up a child in poor housing conditions is no joke

Ordinary People   An account of the plight of the nation's homeless five years after the Housing (Homeless Persons) Act.

Ferndale   A study of a pioneer Shelter/Help the Aged Housing Trust project in South Wales which tackles the acute repair problems faced by elderly home owners.

Homes Wasted   A report on the problem of publicly owned houses standing empty.

Housing aid

Around the country are twenty-nine Housing Aid Centres funded by Shelter. The purpose of these centres is to help people who have housing problems and who have failed to get the help they need from their local council. The workers in the centre often speak on behalf of the families concerned to local official bodies, and endeavour to see that some action is taken. Each year up to 25 000 cases are dealt with in Britain.

Local projects

Giving money to local housing projects is an important part of Shelter's work.

KIRKBY   Kirkby is a council estate on the outskirts of Liverpool. It has a
20   large number of flats which are empty or which have been damaged by

vandals. Shelter's objective here is to work alongside local tenants in an attempt to improve the area. The aim is to have properties either improved or demolished.

LINCOLNSHIRE   Many people think that housing problems exist only in large cities, but housing problems in the country are often as bad as those in cities. Shelter has based a project in the Lincolnshire village of Ludford, with the aim of showing how a community can be improved 'from within'.

In this community, which has less than 150 households, 20 per cent of the houses have no bathroom and 19 per cent have no inside toilet. The idea is to make use of available improvement grants to ensure that everyone in Ludford has somewhere decent to live. (Improvement grants are sums of money given to house owners by the local council to improve their property.) Ludford will then become an example for other communities in the country.

TYNESIDE   In the North-East, Shelter has organized an Education Project. The basic aim is to show local teenagers how they can overcome their own problems in finding decent housing. Using a run-down house as a centre, each week-end a number of school children are taken through the steps any tenant or house owner will face in obtaining or improving their home.

Kirkby

Ludford

The Housing Emergency Office

In towns and cities many houses are left standing empty, sometimes for years. Many of these houses are sound and in good condition, and with a little work could be turned into homes. Shelter's Housing Emergency Office contacts local councils and persuades them to make such houses available on a short-term basis to homeless families in the area. The families pay rent, so the council benefits, and, for a homeless family, being together under a decent roof must seem like heaven.

4
Case Studies

1. Granby, Liverpool

In October 1968 Liverpool City Council agreed to let Shelter begin its Liverpool SNAP (Shelter Neighbourhood Action Project). It was agreed that a group of about 740 houses in Granby, a district of Liverpool, should be the site for the experiment. The aim was to try to improve the whole area. The residents were encouraged to help themselves by taking part in the planning of the improvement schemes.

By July 1969 the people who lived in the area had met together forty-five times. There were three mass meetings, seventeen street group meetings and twenty-five meetings of residents who were concerned with particular aspects of local life such as housing, traffic and vandalism. Exhibitions were set up. A news-sheet was printed. Information on improvement grants was distributed.

Most of the people who lived in Granby liked their houses and did not wish to move. They thought, however, that their homes could be improved by repairs and by the installation of hot water, inside toilets and baths. Within a year of SNAP beginning, 229 applications were made for improvement grants.

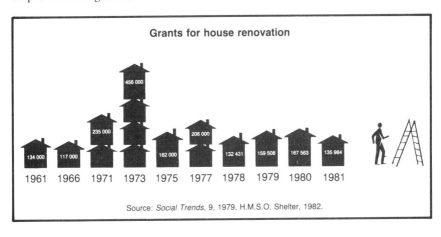

Grants for house renovation

1961	1966	1971	1973	1975	1977	1978	1979	1980	1981
134 000	117 000	235 000	456 000	162 000	206 000	132 431	159 508	167 563	135 984

Source: *Social Trends*, 9, 1979, H.M.S.O. Shelter, 1982.

23

Soon the residents were getting together to discuss all sorts of problems. One problem was prostitution in the area: a local petition was organized against it. Other problems they dealt with were the siting of a telephone-box, unlit back alleys, and the need for containers to dispose of large items of rubbish. An advice centre was set up to give the people of Granby information about the legal aspects of such things as housing, land and divorce.

By this example Shelter showed how an area could improve and care for itself if it was given the right help and advice.

2. The O'Briens

There were four children in the O'Brien family, aged between three and eight. Their father had no job. He was evicted, with the other members of his family, from their council house in Salford because he had been unable to pay the rent. Mr O'Brien explained that this was because he did not know that he could get money for rent from the local Social Security Office.

Salford Council took the children away from their parents after they had been' evicted. They were taken into care and placed with foster parents. Both the children and the parents got on well with the foster parents. The children said they were very kind to them; they bought them new toys and

24   *The O'Brien children*

games and took them on outings. But the children still missed their real parents.

Shelter's Housing Aid Centre in Manchester took up the O'Briens' case. A solicitor, on behalf of Shelter, informed the Council that it would take the matter to court unless the children were returned to their parents. He pointed out to the Council that homelessness is not a sufficient reason in law for a care order. (A care order is when a local council takes a child away from his parents because a court has decided that the parents cannot look after him properly.) Salford dropped the order almost immediately. The children remained in care voluntarily until the family was rehoused.

3. Calderdale

In 1978 Shelter published a report entitled *Where Homelessness Means Hopelessness*. The report was the result of an investigation into how local councils were carrying out the 1977 Housing (Homeless Persons) Act. Under this act every local council has a responsibility to provide permanent housing for certain homeless people and to advise and assist others.

Housing must be provided if a person:

1. is homeless or threatened with homelessness;
2. is within one of a number of 'priority groups', such as families with dependent children, pregnant women, those who are 'at risk' because of old age, and those who are mentally ill or have some physical handicap;
3. has not made himself homeless on purpose.

Shelter's report found that many councils were working hard to help the homeless. A few councils, however, appeared to be avoiding their duty. One such council, according to Shelter, was the Calderdale Council in West Yorkshire. There was, for example, the case of the Midgley family.

Gordon and Joan Midgley and their two children, aged nine and a half and eight, were evicted from their home in Elland by the Halifax Building Society. The Midgleys had been unable to keep up their mortgage repayments. Calderdale Council provided the family with a home for a few weeks and then turned them out although they had nowhere to go. The Council claimed that the Midgleys had made themselves homeless on purpose. Therefore the Housing Department did not have to provide them with a house.

Just over a month after eviction the two children were taken into foster care. Gordon and Joan went from friend to friend and sometimes had to sleep out of doors. Shelter was called in just as the Council was about to have Gordon arrested for not paying the rates on the house in Elland. As a result of pressure from Shelter that house was sold. The family was then reunited in a council house in Rastrick, a small village about five kilometres from Elland.

Shelter maintained that Calderdale Council had not done what it should have done. It had failed to follow the Code of Guidance issued to councils after the passing of the Act. This said that even when homelessness was on purpose, and particulary where children were involved, help should be given to make sure that people in urgent need were not left without shelter. The Code also said that the practice of splitting families was not acceptable.

5

Steve Billcliffe, Shelter Campaigner, Leeds

Interviewer What exactly is your job with Shelter?

S.B. My job is to represent Shelter in Yorkshire and Humberside. My full title is Regional Campaigner.

Interviewer How did you first come to work with Shelter?

S.B. My wife used to work as an assistant in Shelter's office in Newbury. I began working there in my spare time for nothing. When there was a job going in the Newbury office I applied for it, but I wasn't successful. Eventually another job came up and I became a fund-raiser for Shelter in the South-East and Home Counties. I gave talks to schools and organized fund-raising events. Whilst doing this I learnt the skills of giving housing advice and campaigning. I learnt how to get answers out of a local council and how to represent the interests of homeless families. I left the Newbury office when a job came up in Leeds, my home town.

Interviewer What are the housing problems in the West Yorkshire area?

S.B. Immense. When the Labour Government in the mid-seventies began to reduce public spending on housing, it decided to concentrate its funds on areas with very poor housing. There were eight areas in Yorkshire and Humberside which qualified for funds in this way. That gives you some idea of the need in the area.

Interviewer What specific problems are there?

S.B. There are vast waiting-lists for council housing. There's a great number of homeless families. Our idea of homelessness is, of course, rather wide. We include people who live in housing that is not fit for them to live in. There are many slum houses in West Yorkshire. In Leeds, for example, there are about 80 000 houses still standing which 27 were built before the First World War. Of these, 20 000 lack an inside bath and toilet.

Interviewer And what is Shelter doing in the area?

S.B. Our activities are mainly those of campaigning. We see that people are informed about homelessness and we fight for the rights of homeless people. I'm here to keep a close watch on the local councils. I've got to be able to inform the public through television, radio and newspapers where I feel certain local councils are not up to scratch. Very often a local newspaper or television company will come to me because of a story in the news and ask what it means for Yorkshire and Humberside.

Interviewer What other things do you do besides campaigning?

S.B. We do a fair amount of work with local homeless families. At any time in the day I can get a telephone call from Scarborough or Sheffield, Hull or Halifax, and I've got to try to help a family who may be in a very desperate situation. Shelter usually gets the really urgent cases. When the call comes through to the Shelter office, it is likely that the family have tried everywhere else. We often get calls at about three o'clock on a Friday afternoon. That's just when the Housing Department is closing and when they've got nowhere to stay for the weekend.

Interviewer What local project work has Shelter done?

28   *A street in Manningham. The housing improvements can be clearly seen*

S.B. One of the major projects in the West Yorkshire area has been Bradford SHARE (Shelter Housing Aid Renewal Experiment). This began in the late 1960s to improve relations between different races through housing. We gave advice and researched into housing conditions of people living in and near the centre of Bradford. We particularly tried to assist immigrant families, especially those living in a district called Manningham. We helped them fight for better housing conditions. We also worked with the local council on plans for the improvement of whole areas within Manningham. The district had become 'run down' because it was thought that a motorway might run through it. In the end, the council declared part of Manningham a Housing Action Area. This meant that government money could be spent in order to improve the area.

Council workers carrying out improvements in Manningham   29

Interviewer   In Great Britain we have a Welfare State. Why does the State not look after its housing problems and make Shelter unnecessary?

S.B.   We have in this country accepted the basic human right that when you get to the age of five you go to school. We have accepted the basic human right that women should have a vote. We have a health service so that if you get knocked down in the street you receive medical attention. Now, do we accept the basic human right that everyone should have a roof over their head? No. We still regard housing as a reward. The harder you work and the more money you earn, the bigger and better your home. Would people see health care and schooling as a reward? No. We see these as a right. But we still don't see housing as a right.

Steve Billcliffe is no longer a Shelter Campaigner. This interview was recorded before he left Shelter.

6

How Shelter Gets Its Money

Shelter receives no money from the government. It relies on fund-raising and donations to continue its work. There are all kinds of sponsored activities, such as sponsored silences and sponsored swims. In the early days of Shelter, in the mid-1960s, sponsored walks were very popular.

Youth groups seem to have been particularly attracted to raising money for Shelter. Perhaps they were, and still are, attracted by its vision of a reasonable standard of living for everyone.

In 1967 every school and youth club in the country was sent information about Shelter's 'Walk Week'. Altogether 160 walks were organized, most of them by youth groups. Over 6000 young people took part. Perhaps the most ambitious walk was the relay undertaken by forty members of a youth club near Reading: they walked from London to Glasgow – a distance of about 650 kilometres. The following year over 450 walks were organized. Over 40 000 people took part. 'Walk Weeks' were soon bringing

The Donkey Derby at Richmond

in over £100 000 a year and continue to be popular. For example, on 16 June 1979, twenty-one people set off to do a sponsored walk for Shelter across four peaks in the Lake District. Nine finished the whole distance. The event raised over £1600.

Unpaid helpers organize jumble sales, fêtes, house-to-house collections and many other events. For example, the Richmond Shelter Group's annual Donkey Derby is a well-known local event and usually raises over £2500. On 20 June 1979 the Cheshunt and Waltham Cross Shelter Group organized a sponsored cricket match involving a number of well-known people. There was also a raffle of a cricket bat bearing the signatures of the England and Australia cricket teams. The event raised over £1000.

Factories and companies sometimes help too. At Christmas 1978 a firm of estate agents in the West End of London organized a carol concert in aid of Shelter instead of holding their usual Christmas party. The concert raised about £4000.

Donations are Shelter's other source of income. They take many different forms, from a child's pocket-money to a person's promise to give a certain amount each year. However large or small, all are needed and greatly valued.

How each £1 is spent

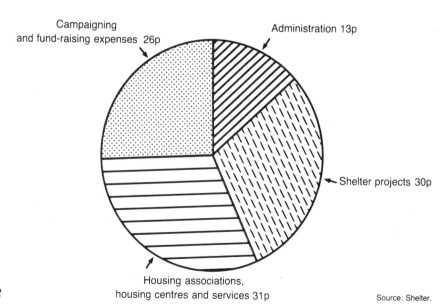

Campaigning and fund-raising expenses 26p

Administration 13p

Shelter projects 30p

Housing associations, housing centres and services 31p

Source: Shelter.

7

The Importance of Shelter

The housing problem is still with us. Families continue to be made homeless. Many more families are still living in terrible conditions. As long as the housing problem remains, Shelter will exist to help those who are unable to help themselves.

Shelter will continue to watch the working of the 1977 Housing Act. It will put pressure on councils which do not appear to be carrying out the Act. It will continue to write its reports, outlining the various causes and results of homelessness. It will fight:

1. to have more houses built;
2. to reduce the waiting-lists for council housing;
3. to have older buildings improved;
4. to stop building societies refusing mortgages on houses in or near a city centre;
5. to improve the management of housing associations;
6. to reduce the number of empty houses;
7. to stop houses being pulled down years before they need to be.

Housing Aid Centres will continue to give advice. Many of them help over a hundred families each week. More money will be given to housing associations. Further local projects will be organized when those in Kirkby and Lincolnshire are past history.

A new project has recently been started in the Rhondda area of Wales. Fifty-one per cent of houses in this area lack such basic items as inside toilets and baths. Elderly people have found it difficult to make improvements to their houses.

Shelter aims to help elderly house owners repair and improve their homes. This should reduce the worries of old people and allow them to remain in the community instead of having to move to old people's homes. First, architects will advise them on what should be done. Then a complete home-repair service will be offered to the most needy in return for a very small fee.

In short, Shelter will continue to care for the homeless. It will continue to fight until everyone has a decent, secure home. Shelter believes that this   *33* dream will come true only when the government and local councils care about the nation's poor and needy.

Shelter's dream can only be a reality when we all care, you and me included.

A family happily rehoused by the Stockport Shelter Housing Action Group

Questions and Projects

A   Comprehension questions

The first few questions are easy, but the later ones are more difficult. Do as many as you can in the time your teacher gives you.

1. When did Shelter start?
2. What was the name of the television play about a homeless mother?
3. What is a 'twilight zone'?
4. What proportion of the population in the U.K. lives in council housing?
5. When did the Conservative Government decide that people could buy council houses?
6. What is Shelter's full name?
7. Where does Shelter take a number of Tyneside teenagers each week-end?
8. Why was Mr O'Brien evicted from his house?
9. Who is Regional Campaigner for Yorkshire and Humberside?
10. How much money does Shelter get from the government?
11. Whom is Shelter helping in the Rhondda area of Wales?
12. What does Shelter's Housing Aid Centre in London do?
13. What is a mortgage?
14. Why is there such a shortage of private rented houses and flats?
15. In what ways are children affected by living in poor housing?
16. What is 'multiple occupation'?
17. What are 'improvement grants'?
18. How did the Bradford SHARE project help immigrant families?
19. For what seven things will Shelter continue to fight?
20. Explain why the solicitor acting for Mr O'Brien threatened to take Salford Council to court.

B   Discussion topics

Divide into small groups of five or six. Discuss the following questions and appoint someone to write down your ideas, reasons and conclusions.
1. Why do people become homeless? Is it their own fault?
2. Should council houses be sold to tenants? Set out the arguments for and against.
3. A thirteen-year-old boy wrote in an essay that a 'house' was different from a 'home'. What do you think he meant? What are the differences between the two?

35

4. What advice would you give to a couple with two young children who have become homeless?

5. What sort of house or flat would you like to live in? Do you think it would be better to buy or to rent it? Give your reasons.

C Activities

Here are some ideas for learning through activities.

1. Visit an area of bad housing near to your school or home and make a sketch of some of the houses there.

2. Compare the housing conditions in two different areas. One should be an area of poor housing. You should note in each case:
    (a) the number of well-kept houses in the street;
    (b) the number of badly kept houses in the street;
    (c) the number of well-kept gardens in the street;
    (d) the number of badly kept gardens in the street;
    (e) other features of the street (litter, corner shops, stray dogs, groups of people talking, vandalism, etc.).

3. Choose four members of your class to be the local housing committee. The remainder of the class should divide into groups. Each group should present a case for an imaginary family to be given a council house. Unfortunately, there are not enough council houses to go round. The housing committee has to select which families should be offered the council houses.

4. Design and plan a new council estate. Your estate should include housing, shops, a community centre, a church, a public house, a cinema, areas of green or parkland, and any other facilities you think necessary.

D Practical work

Here are some suggestions as to how *you* can help Shelter. Talk them over with your teacher or parents.

1. Organize a sponsored event for Shelter.

2. Make a display of classwork, surveys, photographs, etc. on homelessness and the work of Shelter. Put it up on a notice-board in your school's display area.

3. Find out what your local council is doing for those living in bad housing and for those who are homeless. You can do this by looking for reports in local newspapers and by writing to the local housing committee at your Civic Hall, Town Hall or Guildhall. You will find the address in your local telephone directory.

E   Essays

Use you own words to write essays on the following subjects. You will find some of the books mentioned in the next section helpful.
1. Outline the various sorts of work done by Shelter.
2. (a) Explain the causes and consequences of homelessness.
   (b) Outline the provisions of two Acts of Parliament dealing with housing.
3. Describe the housing problems in a district known to you. Suggest ways in which they could be overcome and what help could be given by a local church or organization.

Resource Material

A list of addresses is given at the end.

BOOKS
(P) *Annual Progress Report* (Shelter)
(P) *Housing* by Francis Leigh (Edward Arnold)
(P) *Housing Facts and Figures* (Shelter)
(P) *No Place to Grow Up* (Shelter)
(P) *Somewhere to Live* by D. Church and B. Ford (Nelson)
(T) *Where Homelessness Means Hopelessness* (Shelter)

(P) = suitable for pupils
(T) = suitable for teachers

TEACHING PACKS
Tenement A simulation game which illustrates the difficulties faced by families when dealing with all kinds of housing situations. (For pupils in fifth forms.)
Street A housing project containing a variety of material including facsimile letters, official notices, Department of the Environment leaflets and charts, a cassette tape and a simulation game.

Both packs available from Shelter.

WALLCHARTS
Two posters illustrating different aspects of housing in Britain are available from Shelter.

FILMS
Cathy Come Home 82 min., black and white. The famous BBC film mentioned in this booklet.
What Can Be Done 33 min., colour. Shelter's film about housing problems and their solution.

Both films available from Concord Films Council Ltd.

FILMSTRIPS
Housing Commentary on either tape or cassette. Available for purchase from the National Audio-Visual Aids Library.
Housing and Society (The Media Production Company) Commentary on cassette. Available from The Slide Centre Ltd.

ADDRESSES

Concord Films Council Ltd, 201 Felixstowe Road, Ipswich, Suffolk IP3 9BJ.
National Audio-Visual Aids Library, Paxton Place, Gipsy Road, London
    SE27 9SR.
Shelter, 157 Waterloo Road, London SE1 8XF.
The Slide Centre Ltd, 143 Chatham Road, London SW11 6SR.

DERBYSHIRE

SAINT BENEDICT
SCHOOL

COUNTY COUNCIL